ISBN
978-1-965005-34-7
© Carlos Maldonado 2024

Page Intentionally Left Blank

# D Major Scale Studies
# Re

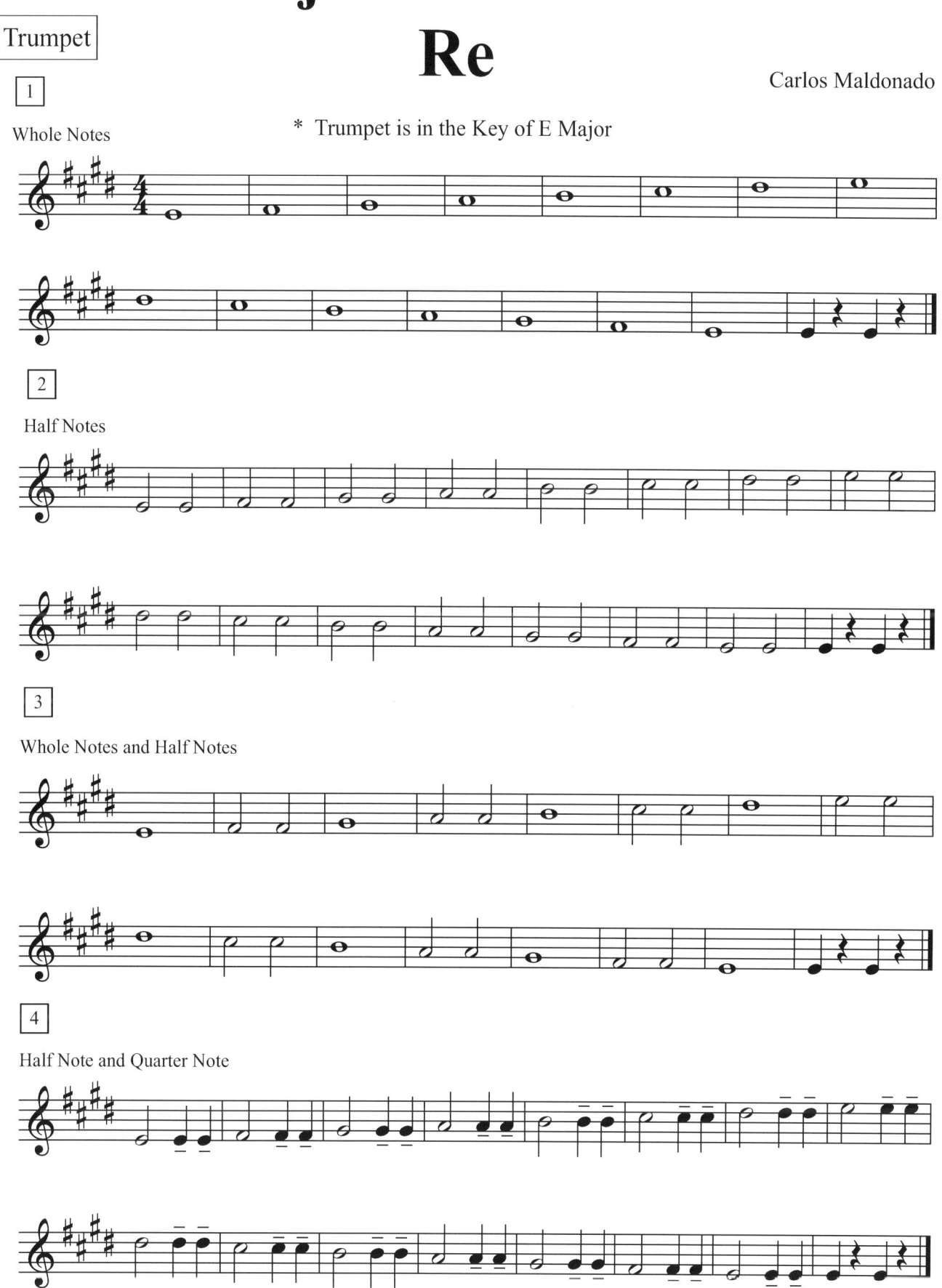

**Trumpet**

Carlos Maldonado

* Trumpet is in the Key of E Major

**1**

Whole Notes

**2**

Half Notes

**3**

Whole Notes and Half Notes

**4**

Half Note and Quarter Note

©Maldonado Publishing 2023

## 5
Half Note and Quarter Note

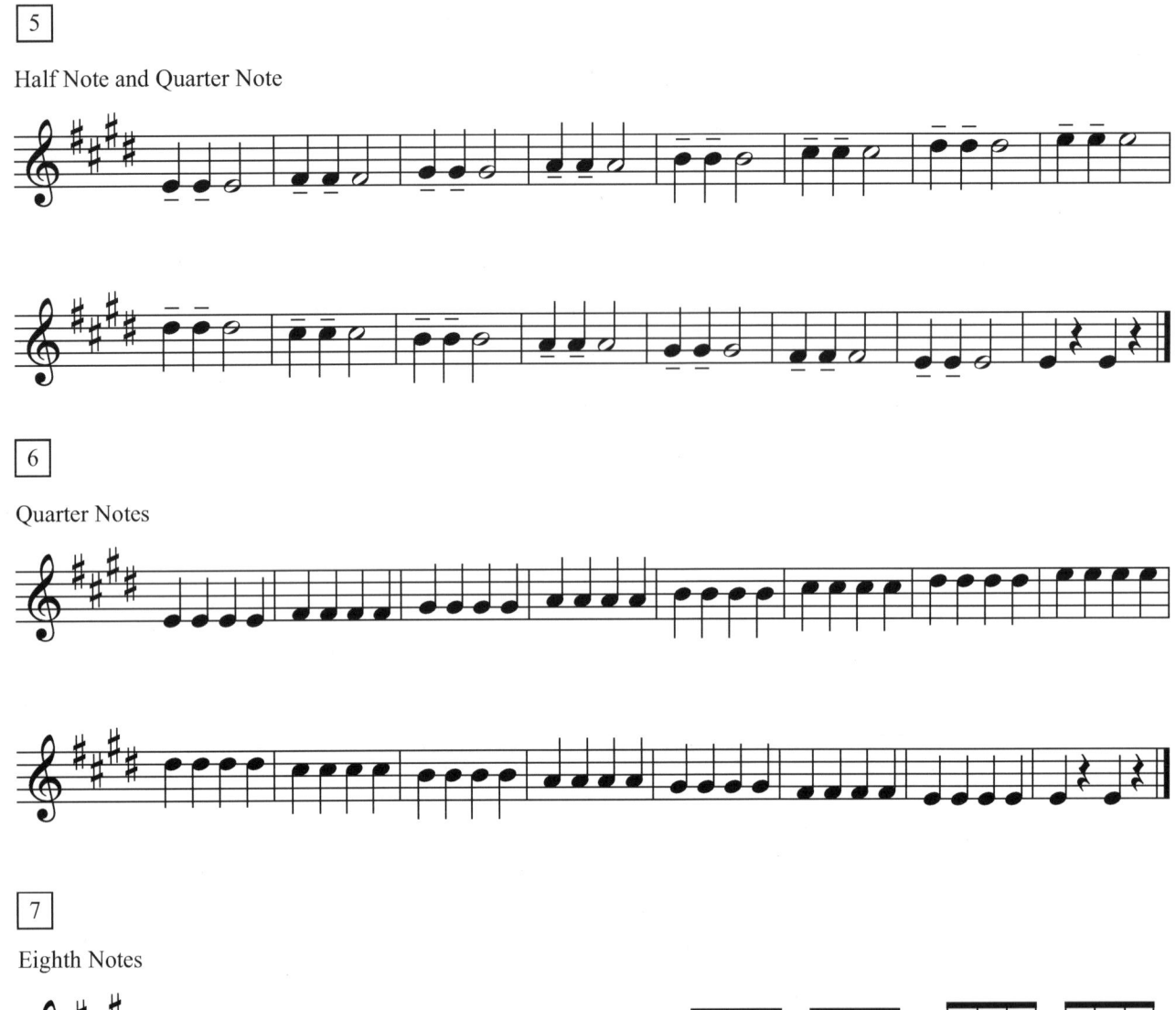

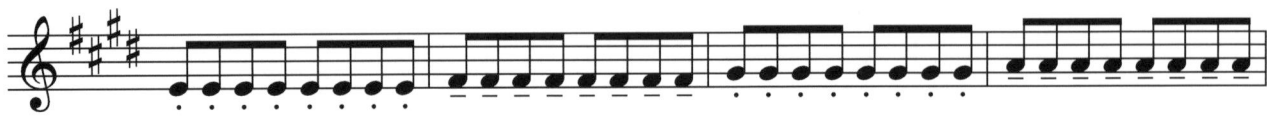

## 6
Quarter Notes

## 7
Eighth Notes

**8**

Quarter Notes and Eighth Notes 1

**9**

Quarter Notes and Eighth Notes 2

## 10

Quarter Notes and Eighth Notes 3

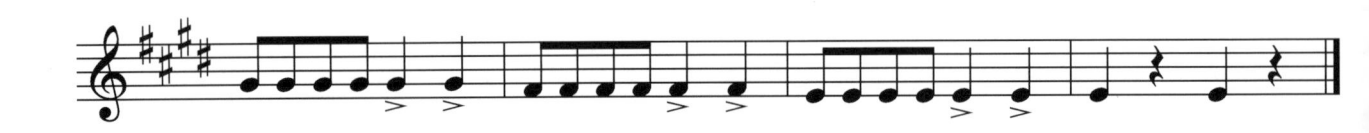

## 11

Quarter Notes and Eighth Notes 4

**12**

Quarter Notes and Eighth Notes 5

**13**

Quarter Notes and Quarter Rest 1

**14**

Quarter Notes and Quarter Rest 2

## 15

Quarter Notes, Eighth Notes and Rest

## 16

Sixteenth Notes

## 17
Sixteenth Notes and Eighth Notes

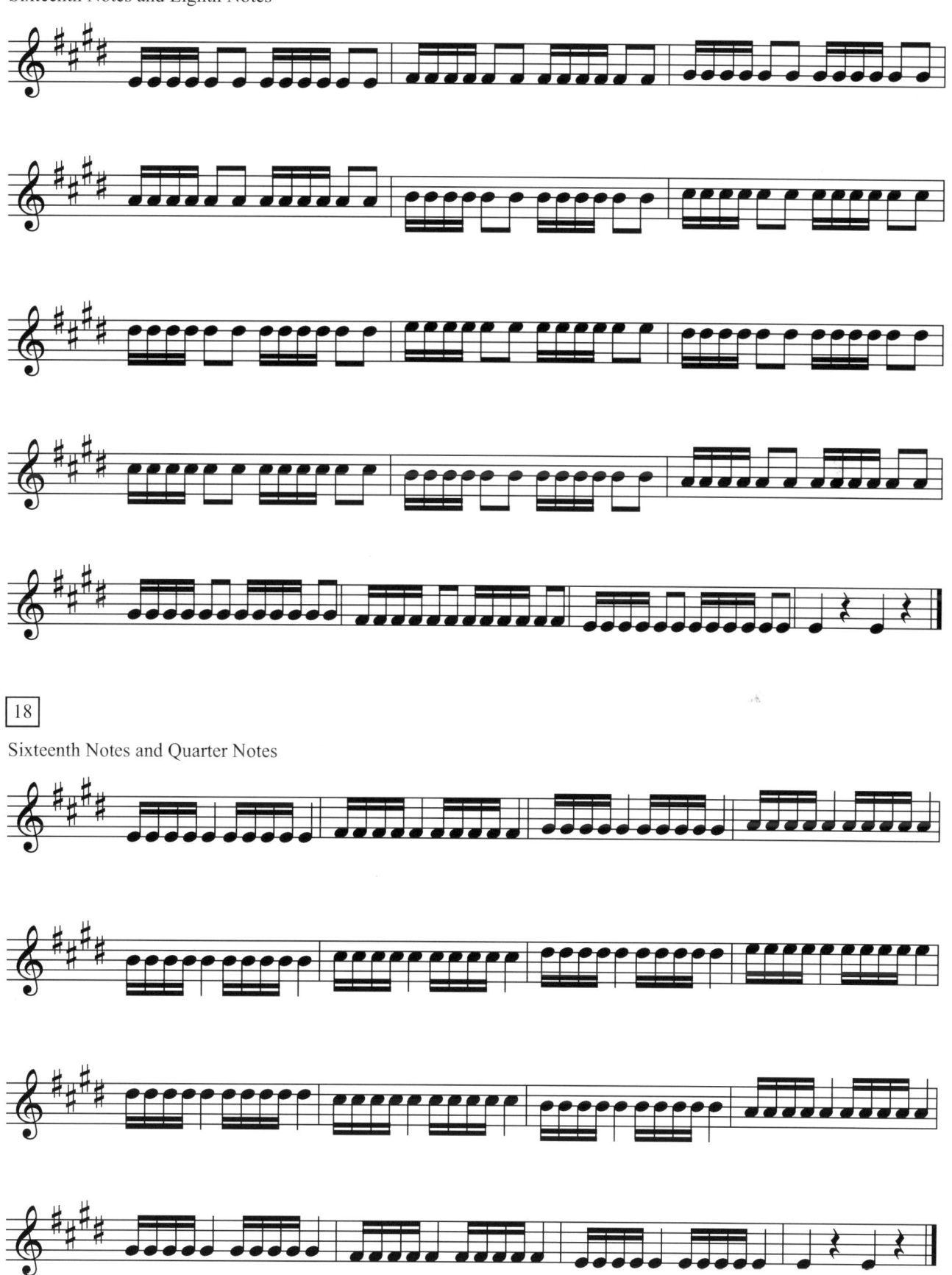

## 18
Sixteenth Notes and Quarter Notes

### 19
Tadimi

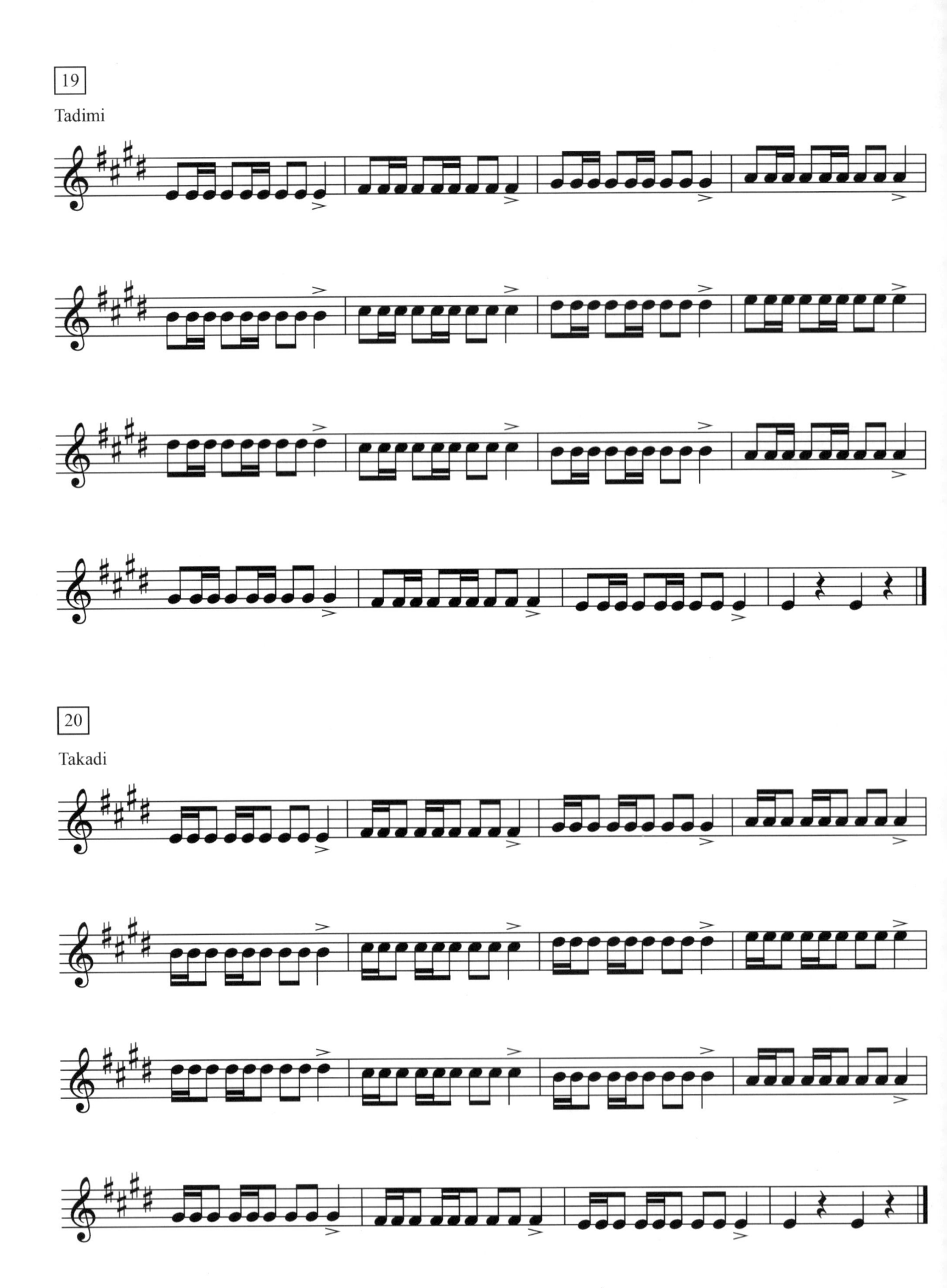

### 20
Takadi

**21**

Dotted Half Note 1

**22**

Dotted Half Note 2

**23**

Dotted Quarter Note 1

**24**

Dotted Half Note 2

**25**

Dotted Eighth Note 1

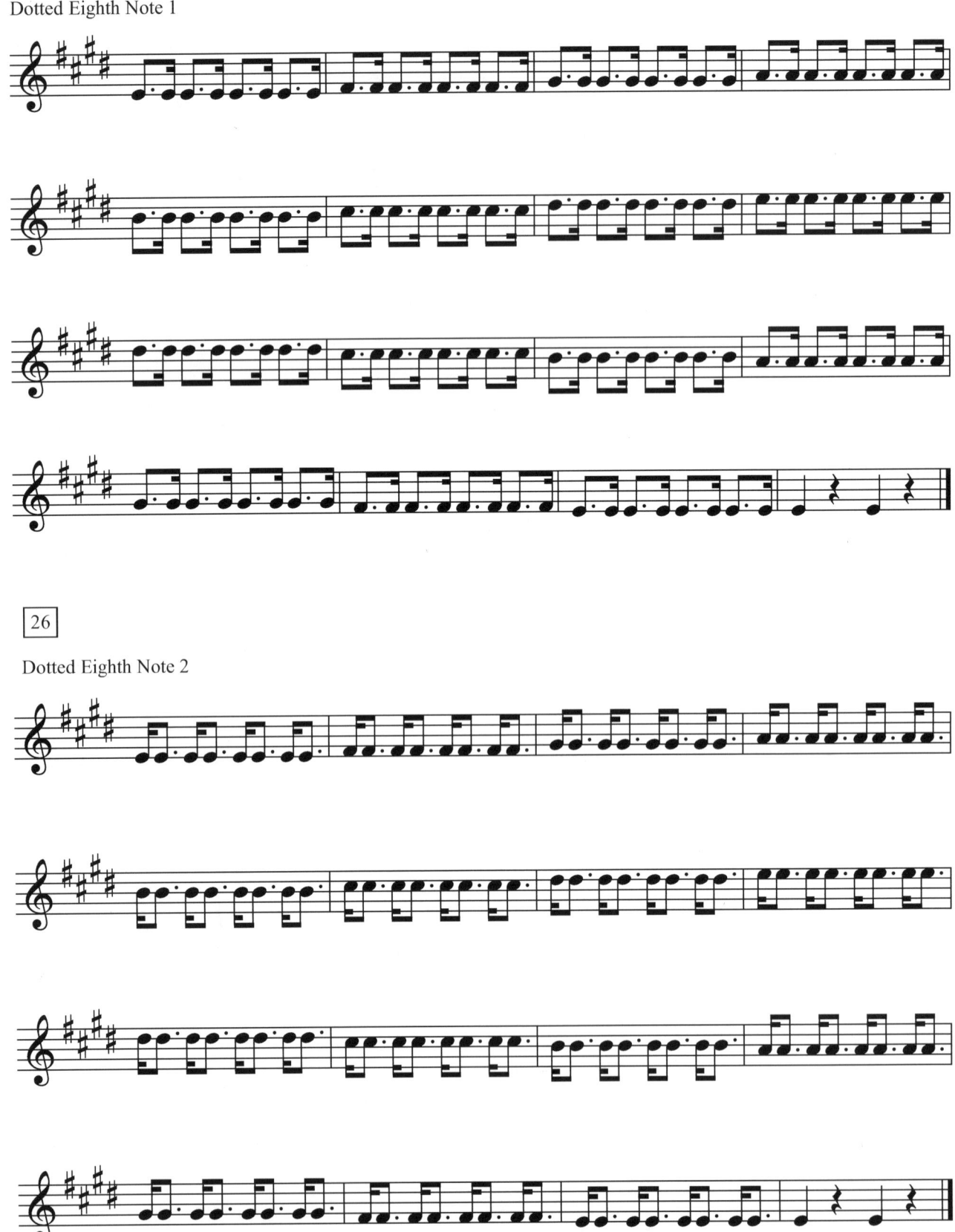

**26**

Dotted Eighth Note 2

27

Syncopation 1

28

Syncopation 2

## 29

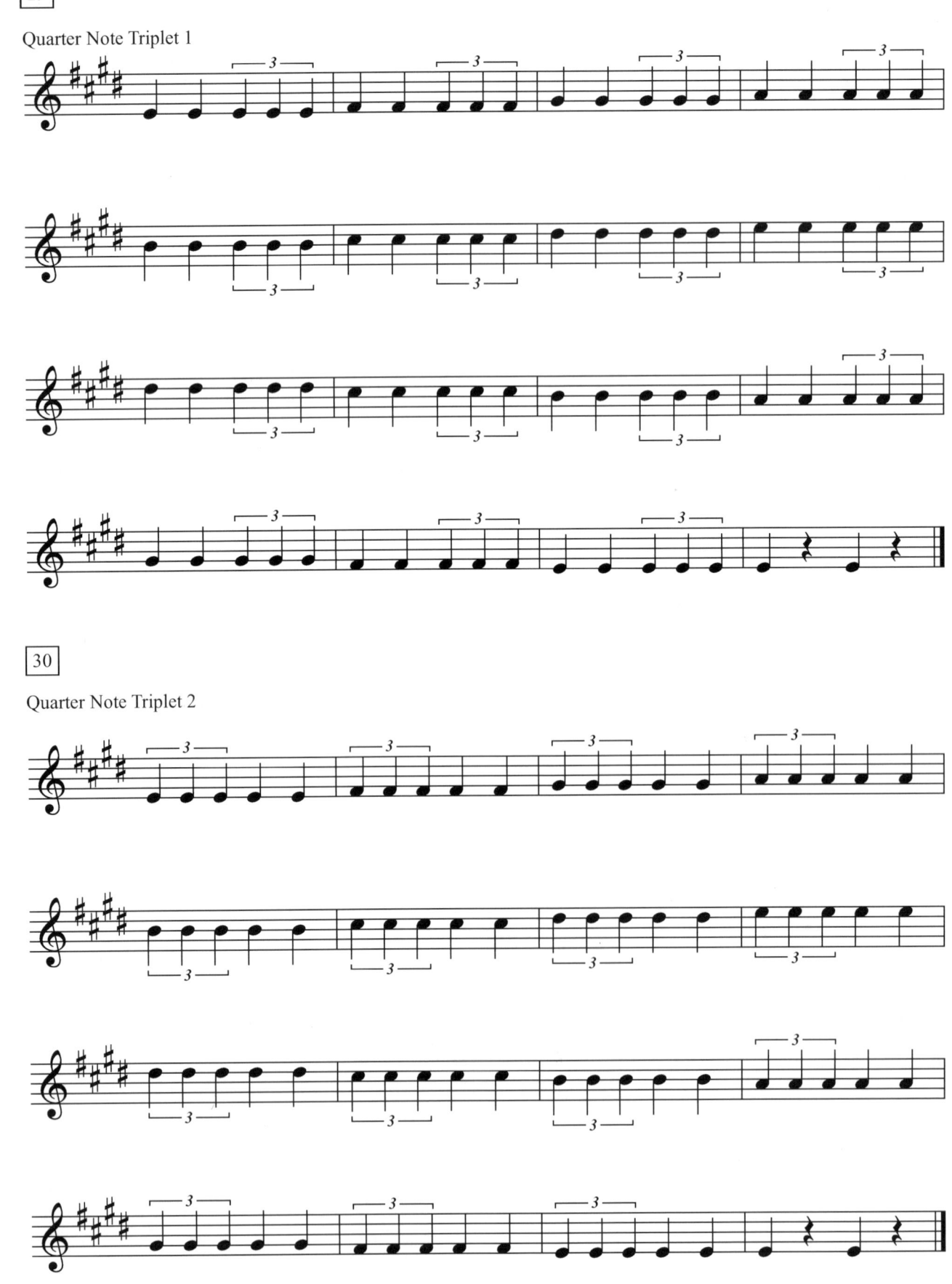

Quarter Note Triplet 1

## 30

Quarter Note Triplet 2

**31**

Eighth Note Triplet

**32**

D Major In 3rds

**33**

Quarter Note Scale Study

**34**

Half Note and Quarter Note Scale Study

**35**

Eighth Note and Quarter Note Scale Study

**36**

Dotted Quarter Note Scale Study

**37**

3rd Position Scale Study 1

**38**

3rd Position Scale Study 2

**39**

3rd Position Scale Study 3

**40**

3rd Position Scale Study 4

**41**

3rd Position Scale Study 5

**42**

Shifting to III and IV Position 1

**43**

Shifting to III and IV Position 2

**44**

Shifting to III and IV Position 3

## 45

Shifting to III and IV Position 4

## 46

Shifting to III and IV Position 5

## 47

Dotted Half Note

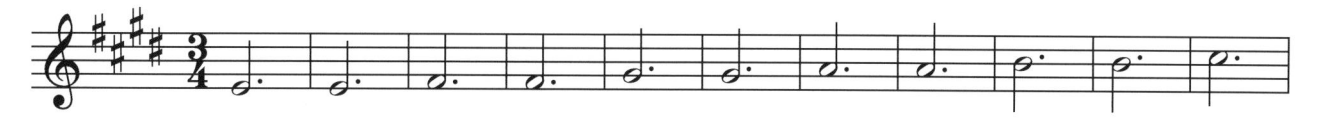

**48**

Quarter Notes

**49**

Half Note and Quarter Note 1

**50**

Half Note and Quarter Note 2

**51**

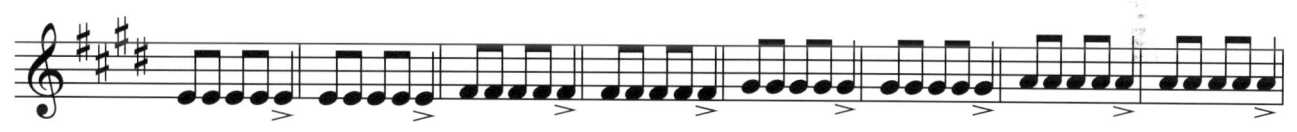

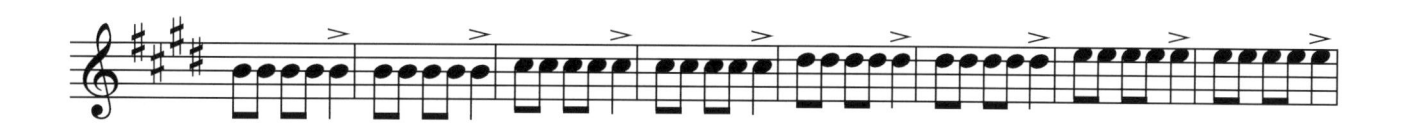

Quarter Notes and Eighth Notes 1

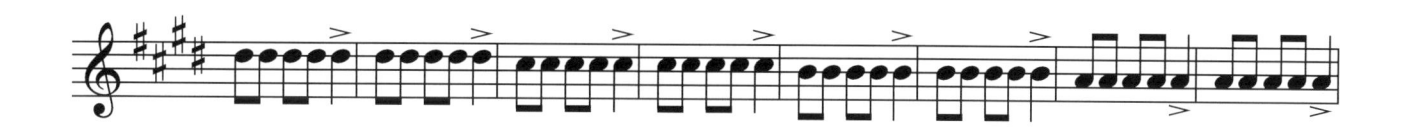

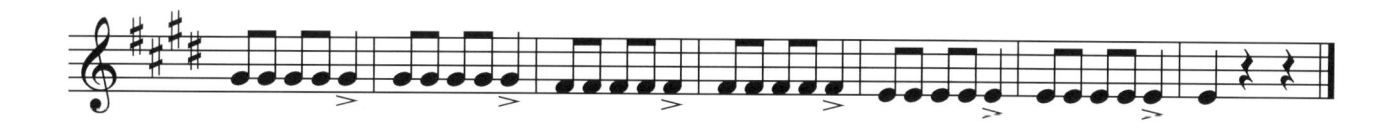

## 52
Quarter Notes and Eighth Notes 2

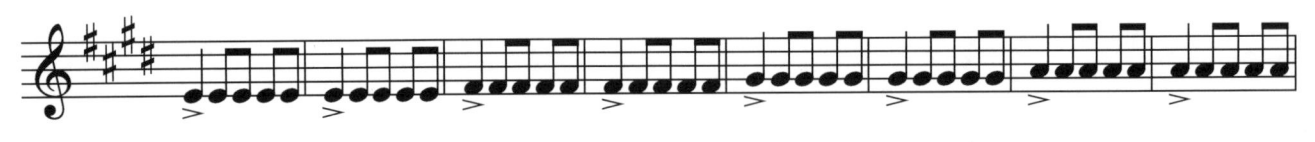

## 53
Quarter Notes and Eighth Notes 3

**54**

Eighth Notes

**55**

Dotted Quarter Note 1

## 56
Dotted Quarter Note 2

## 57
Dotted Quarter Note 3

**58**

Syncopation 1

**59**

Syncopation 2

**60**

D Major In 3rds

**61**

Quarter Note Scale Study

**62**

Half Note and Quarter Note Scale Study

**63**

Eighth Note and Quarter Note Scale Study

**64**

3rd Position Scale Study 1

**65**

3rd Position Scale Study 2

## 66

3rd Position Scale Study 3

## 67

3rd Position Scale Study 4

## 68

**Shifting to III and IV Position 1**

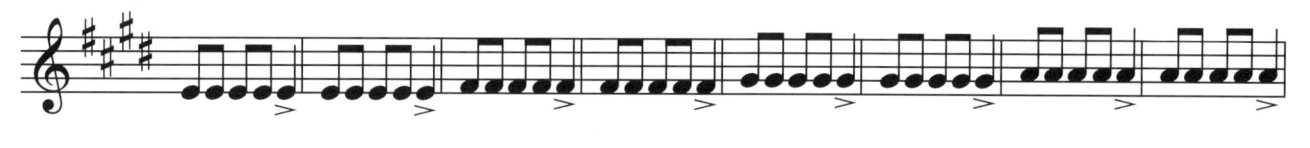

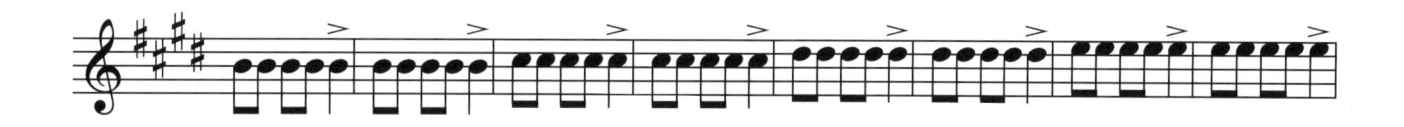

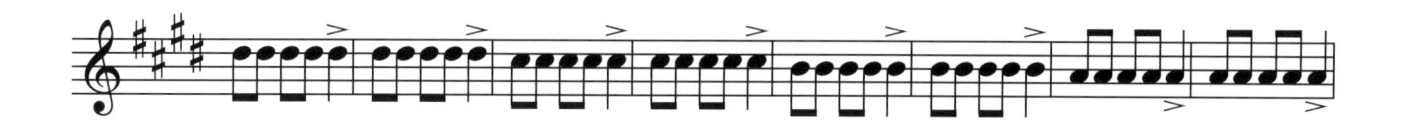

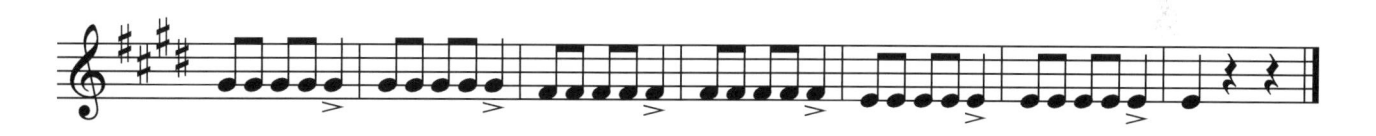

## 69

**Shifting to III and IV Position 2**

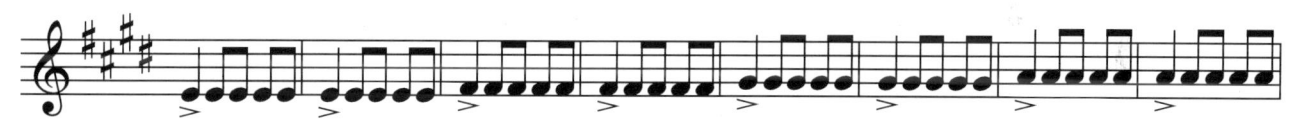

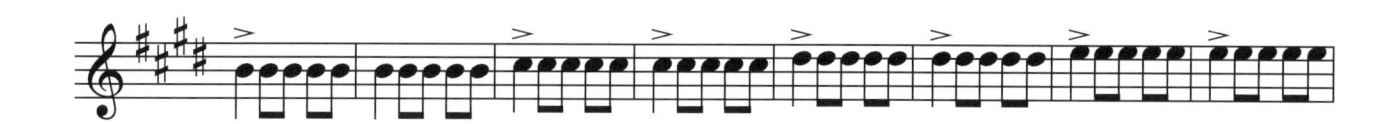

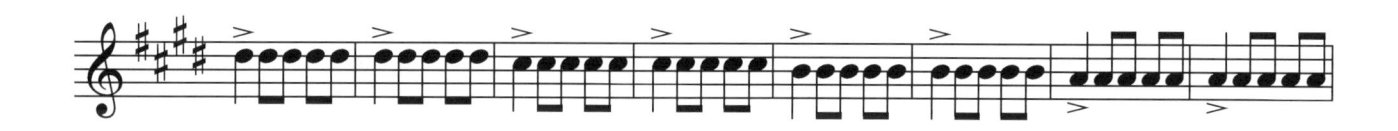

**70**

Shifting to III and IV Position 3

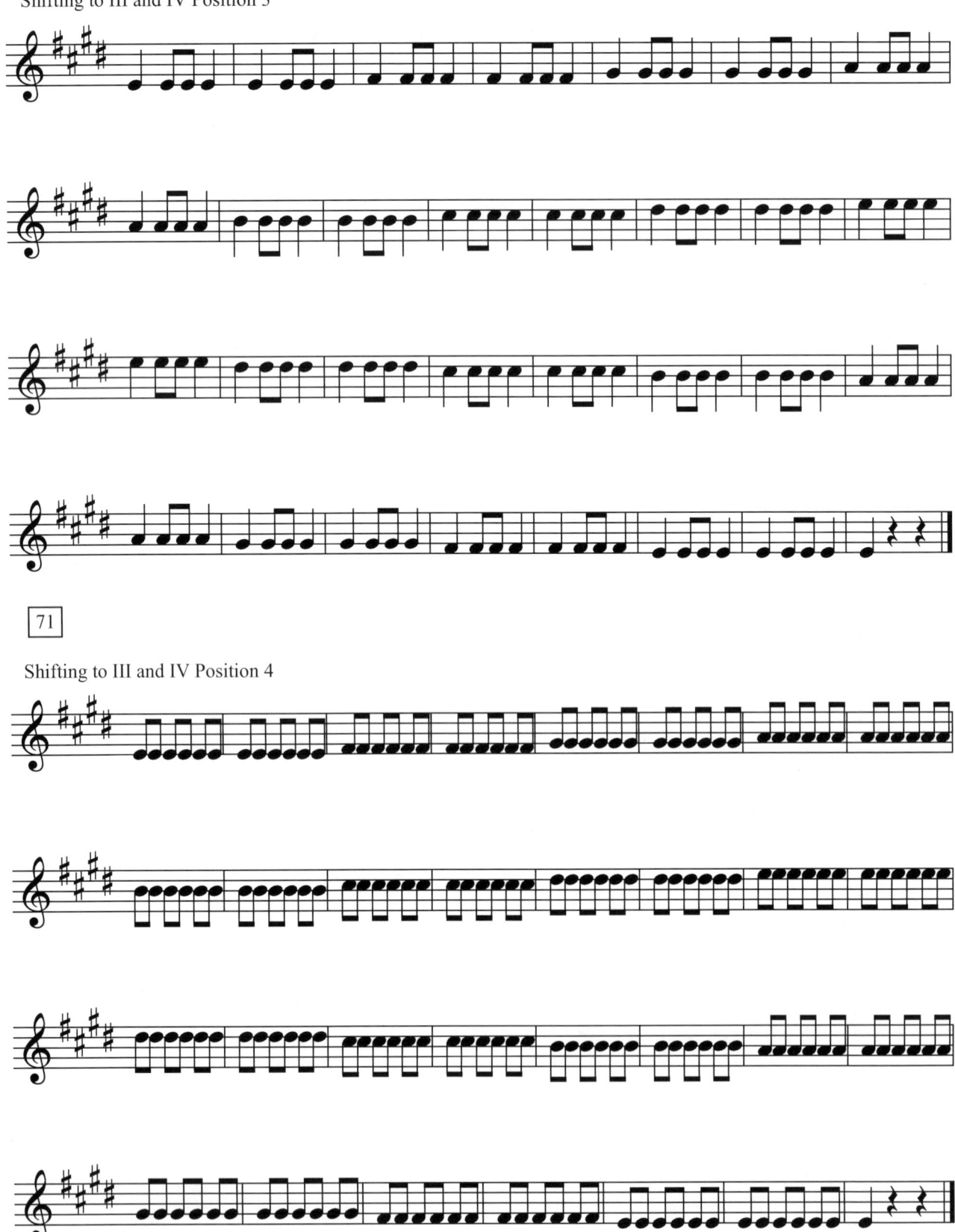

**71**

Shifting to III and IV Position 4

**72**

Half Notes

**73**

Half Note and Quarter Note 1

**74**

Half Note and Quarter Note 2

## 75
Quarter Notes

## 76
Eighth Notes

## 77
Quarter Notes and Eighth Notes 1

### 78
Quarter Notes and Eighth Notes 2

### 79
Quarter Notes and Eighth Notes 3

### 80
Quarter Notes and Eighth Notes 4

**81**

Quarter Notes and Eighth Notes 5

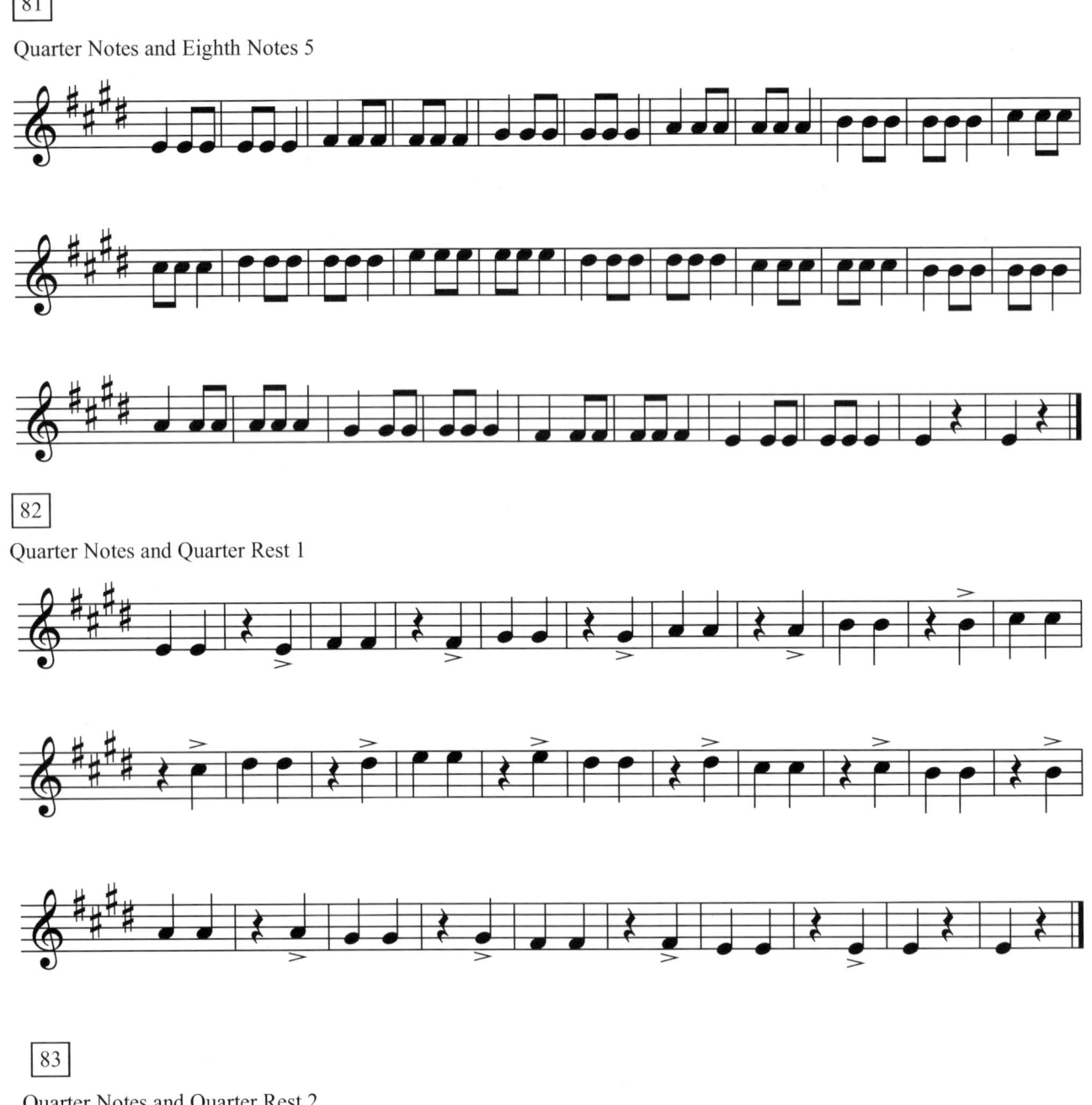

**82**

Quarter Notes and Quarter Rest 1

**83**

Quarter Notes and Quarter Rest 2

## 84
Quarter Notes, Eighth Notes and Rest

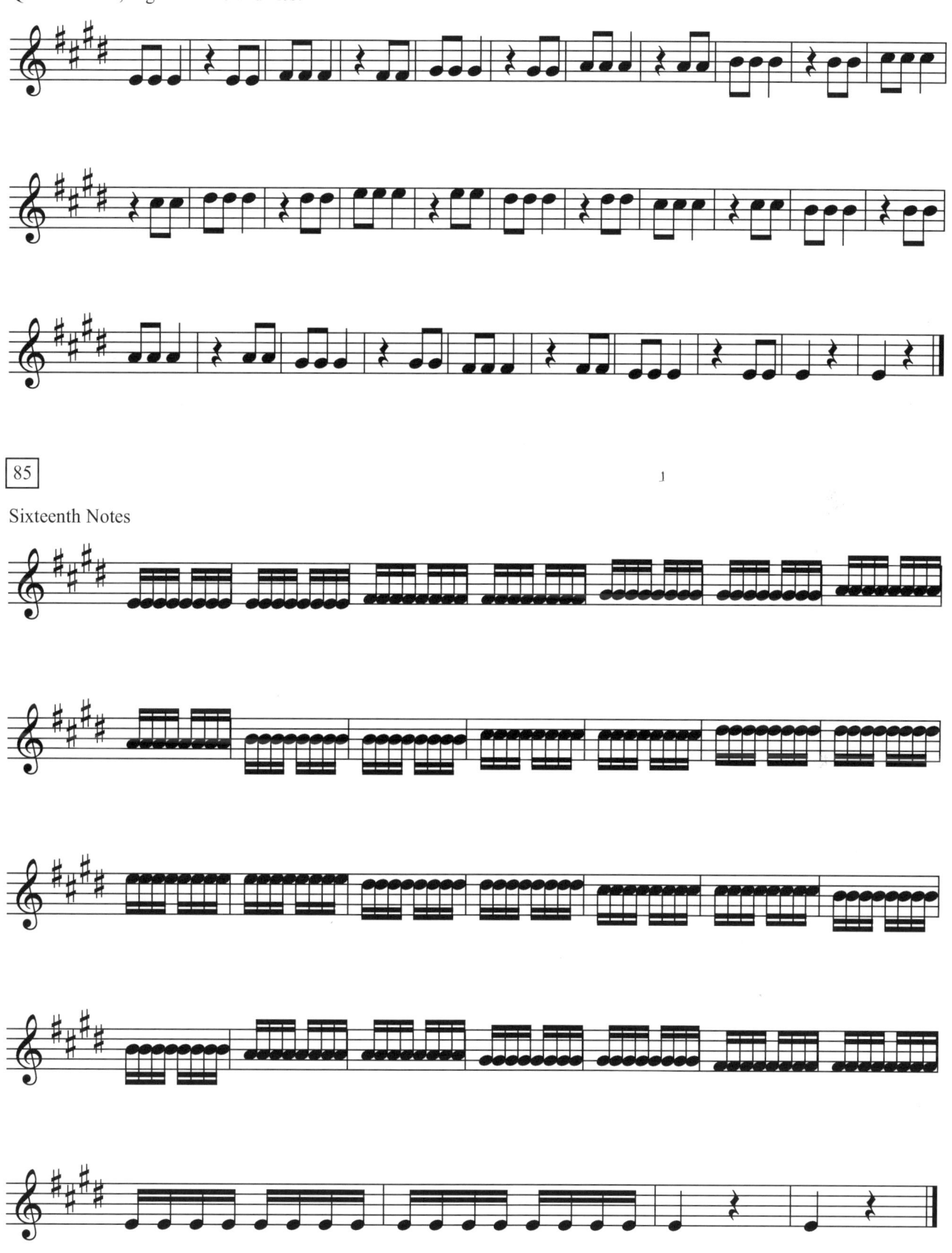

## 85
Sixteenth Notes

## 86
**Sixteenth Notes and Eighth Notes**

## 87
**Sixteenth Notes and Quarter Notes**

## 88
Tadimi

## 89
Takadi

## 90

Half Note and Quarter Note Tie 1

## 91

Half Note and Quarter Note Tie 2

**92**

Dotted Quarter Note 1

**93**

Dotted Quarter Note 2

**94**

Dotted Eighth Note 1

**95**

Dotted Eighth Note 2

**96**

Syncopation 1

**97**

Syncopation 2

## 98
Quarter Note Triplet 1

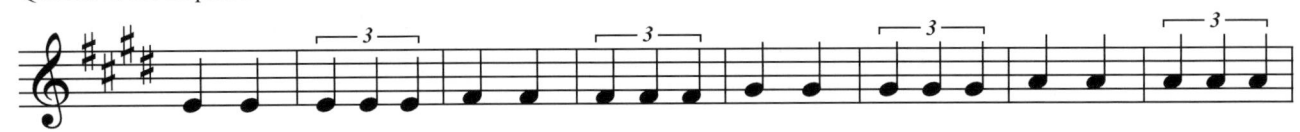

## 99
Quarter Note Triplet 2

**100**

Eighth Note Triplet

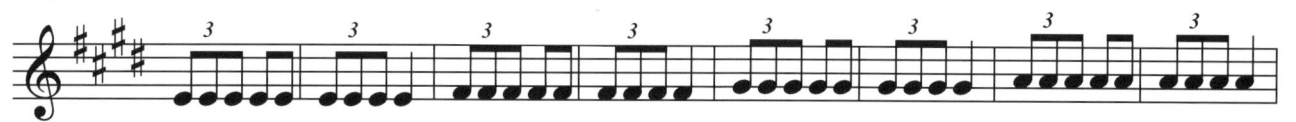

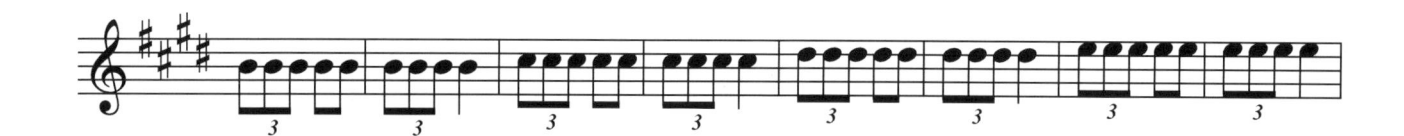

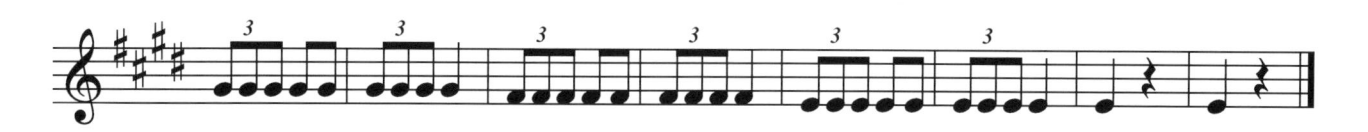

**101**

D Major In 3rds

**102**

Quarter Note Scale Study

**103**

Half Note and Quarter Note Scale Study

**104**

Eighth Note and Quarter Note Scale Study

**105**

Dotted Quarter Note Scale Study

**106**

3rd Position Scale Study 1

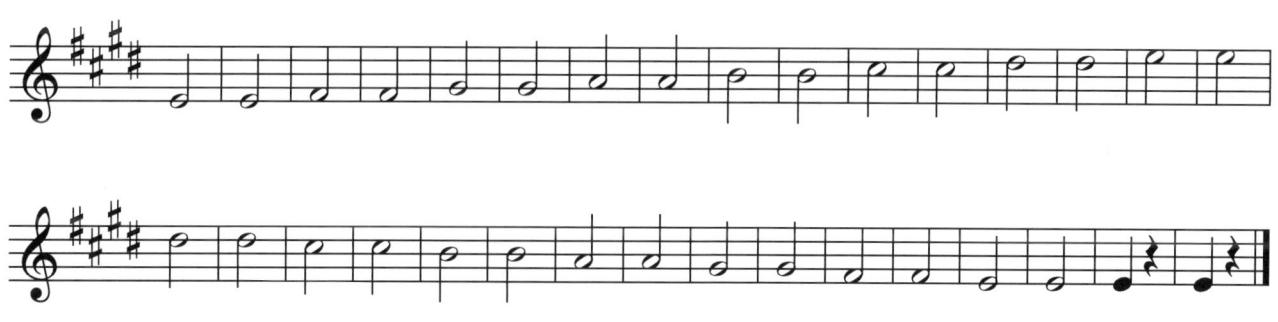

**107**

3rd Position Scale Study 2

**108**

3rd Position Scale Study 3

**109**

3rd Position Scale Study 4

**110**

3rd Position Scale Study 5

**111**

Shifting to III and IV Position 1

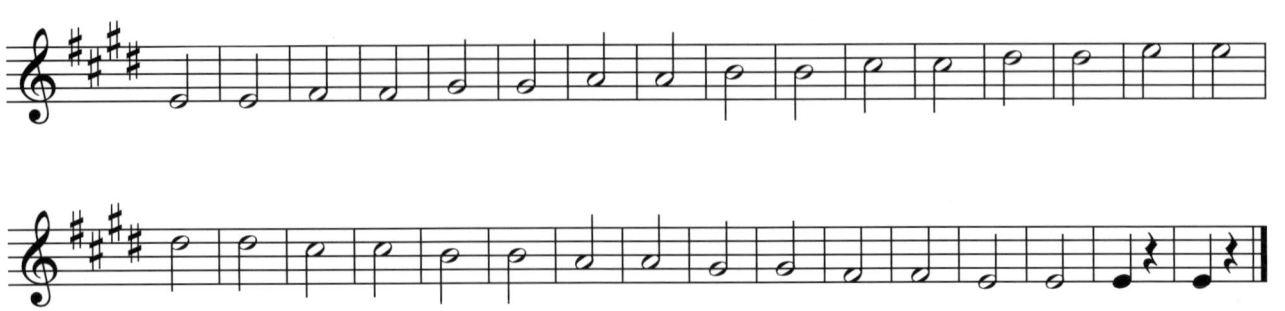

**112**

Shifting to III and IV Position 2

**113**

Shifting to III and IV Position 3

**114**

Shifting to III and IV Position 4

**115**

Shifting to III and IV Position 5

Made in the USA
Columbia, SC
29 September 2024